THE SOIL AND WATER BALANCE

The Science Behind Soil Friendly Farming

Game & Wildlife
CONSERVATION TRUST

First published in Great Britain in 2018 by
Game & Wildlife Conservation Trading Ltd
Burgate Manor, Fordingbridge SP6 1EF
www.gwct.org.uk

A catalogue record for this book is available from the
British Library.

First printed February 2018.

978-1-901369-29-8

Written by Jennifer Brewin.
Designed and typeset in Minion Pro
by James Swyer.

Front cover © danm12/Shutterstock
Inside front cover © GWCT

FOREWORD

"The thin layer of soil covering the earth's surface represents the difference between survival and extinction for most terrestrial life"
- Doran and Parkin, 1994.

Despite this statement, the soil beneath our feet is often overlooked and undervalued.

Soil underpins human health and wellbeing, thanks to the diverse range of goods and services soils deliver to society. For example, the Food and Agriculture Organization of the United Nations state that over 97% of our food comes from soil. Global warming can be offset by storing carbon in soil. Flooding risks can be controlled when soils absorb heavy rainfall. These, and many other soil-derived benefits, are directly related to individual and national economic status.

As such, a better understanding of soils, and their properties, processes and functions is essential, if this vital, yet virtually finite component of natural capital is to be appreciated and protected.
Over many years, the Allerton Project's soils research programmes have contributed to much of this understanding. Collaborative research at Loddington continues to provide long-term, robust scientific evidence on soils and soil health, at field, farm and catchment scales. Importantly, this extensive knowledge is gathered in a real, working environment and supports the development, demonstration and adoption of effective, economically-viable and sustainable soil management policies and practices.

As well as generating this valuable evidence, the Allerton Project ensures soils research has real impact to many beneficiaries. The scientific knowledge and technical skills of Project staff are shared with a wide range of stakeholders, from school children to researchers to Government ministers. Working closely with these key stakeholders ensures soil and soil management research at the Allerton Project continues to find appropriate solutions to the economic, regulatory and environmental uncertainties that farmers face now, and into the future.

Professor Jane Rickson,
Chair in Soil Erosion and Conservation

Cranfield Soil and AgriFood Institute,
Cranfield University, Cranfield, UK
January 2018

PREFACE

"Man – despite his artistic pretension, his sophistication and his many accomplishments – owes his existence to a 15cm layer of topsoil and the fact that it rains" - Anon.

Throughout the last century, farming has changed dramatically. A 1920s farmer would not recognise the modern, high-tech, high productivity environment of today's farm. With these advances came enormous and much needed increases in yield from the post-war years to the latter part of the 20th century, however across the UK yields have been plateauing and even falling over the past 30 years. This shows that although the techniques that have allowed high output farming revolutionised the industry, they perhaps do not care sufficiently for the fundamental components that support us, such as the soil. Soil structure, organic matter and overall soil health have been in decline, and we must address these issues if we wish to achieve sustainable farming.

The challenge we now face is to maintain profitable and productive farming, whilst reversing these effects. There is much that can be done to benefit farm businesses whilst reducing the negative impact of modern agriculture on the environment when it comes to soil and water. Keeping the soil on the fields, preventing nutrients and chemicals from travelling into water courses and valuing soil structure are initial steps towards a more sustainable approach. With the knowledge we now have from our research, we can certainly make progress in improving these areas.

We know that many farmers are enthusiastic about these advances, and would be prepared to adjust their farming practices. However, where these adjustments come with a cost, increased uptake needs to be encouraged by financial support for such measures. Many are simple and cost-efficient enough to be included in agri-environment schemes, and supporting these through forward-looking policy will encourage many more to take positive steps towards sustainable soil management.

The GWCT's Allerton Project has been involved in many research projects with many partners over the last 25 years. These examine water quality, soil health, impacts on crop yield, and how we might reduce the impact of modern farming methods on the environment, whilst maintaining food production and an economic business model for the farm. The knowledge gained from some of these studies has recently been brought together into our ongoing Water Friendly Farming project, which combines these separate threads into a practical, landscape scale demonstration. This document explores the main findings from our research projects, discusses what we have learnt, and considers how our findings might be applied in the future.

This report does not mark the end of our work. We have new projects underway that will yield further important results over the next five years. There is a lot that remains to be done, but after 15 years of scientific research into farming techniques at the GWCT's Allerton Project and elsewhere, we are in a stronger position to make responsible choices towards sustainable farming.

CONTENTS

WHY IS SOIL RESEARCH SO IMPORTANT?

- Soil is precious. It is critical for life. We are currently losing millions of tonnes of arable topsoil each year in the UK to erosion[1], but we cannot replace it. The formation of even a centimetre of soil takes thousands of years. **p26.**
- As our soils degrade, our ability to grow food, support wildlife and store carbon and water are compromised.
- Healthy soil represents a very large store of carbon – the top 30cm alone is thought to contain more than twice as much carbon as there is in carbon dioxide in the atmosphere[2]. **p17.**
- The effects of erosion are often felt more severely at the site the soil is deposited, rather than where it is eroded from. This is one reason the problem is not prioritised. **p25.**
- Sediment is one the biggest problems facing freshwater bodies and fisheries in the UK. **p27.**
- Agriculture is thought to contribute 70% of the nitrogen and 28% of the phosphorus in UK waters[3]. **p39.**
- Up to 95% of water bodies in the UK have raised levels of nitrogen, and in agricultural areas the levels are high enough to be ecologically damaging in most streams[4]. **p39.**
- Raised levels of nutrients and sediment in rivers can have many consequences, including: sediment smothering fish eggs and depriving them of oxygen, sunlight not penetrating as far into water ecosystems, and waterways becoming choked with algae and weed. **Section 1.4.**

WHAT HAVE WE LEARNT SO FAR?

- Ploughing disrupts natural soil structure and reduces organic matter, so reducing or avoiding ploughing can help preserve structure and preserve organic material in soil. **p20**.

- Reduced or no-tillage farming can decrease the amount of surface runoff and erosion (by up to 90% on some plots), improve soil structure and workability, and increase soil health and organic matter. However, it is not suitable everywhere – some crops, soil types, climates can be more challenging. **p46**.

- More runoff and erosion comes along field tramlines than from the cropped area. This can be reduced by using low pressure tyres, or methods to break up the soil surface in the tramline. Some capital grants are already available to support these techniques. **p54**.

- Cover crops protect and improve the soil, and add nutrients as "green manure". In the right circumstances cover crops can reduce erosion by sheltering the soil, reduce weeds over winter and in the following crop, and improve soil organic matter content. **p50**.

- Conservation Agriculture combines reduced tillage, ground cover and good crop rotation. It can have many benefits for soil, biodiversity and the farmer, but there may be drawbacks. A change of farming practice requires planning, a good understanding of soils and technology as well as a change in mind-set. **p68**.

- Agriculture is the main overall source of phosphorus in rivers, but during the biologically sensitive times of spring, summer and early autumn, most phosphorus comes from domestic sources[5]. This could be addressed – 80% of septic tanks are probably working inefficiently[6]. **p66**.

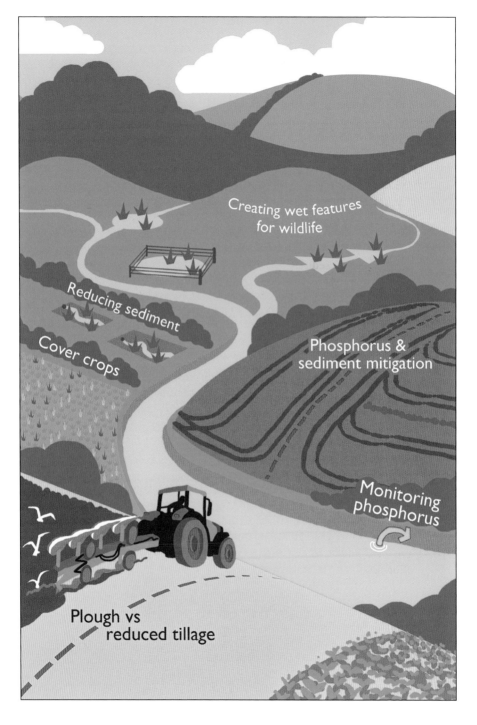

Ploughing vs reduced tillage was studied in the *SOWAP* project, to examine the impact of reduced or no-tillage on many factors including soil health, soil erosion, nutrient loss from fields and biodiversity.

Phosphorus was monitored in the streams running through several different catchment areas in the *PARIS* project. These differed in farming practices, and we studied the impact of the farming itself and other factors such as sewage treatment on river phosphorus and biodiversity.

Phosphorus and sediment mitigation measures have been studied in two projects at Allerton. *MOPS1*, which looked for ways to reduce sediment and phosphorus loss using tramline management, beetle banks and reduced tillage. The *Tramlines* project followed on from this, and examined in more detail how tramlines can be managed to reduce sediment loss.

Cover crops were studied in the *SIP* project, which looked at the effect of different cover crop species on soil biology, chemistry and physics, and the effect on weed growth.

Reducing sediment. Field wetlands were studied for their ability to reduce sediment in field runoff water in the *MOPS2* project.

Wet features for wildlife were created in the wetting up *farmland for biodiversity* project, which examined the importance of such features for birds and insects in a farmland landscape

More detail about all these projects and their findings is shown in section 6.

Illustration © Chris Heward

1. THE PROBLEMS

1.1 SOIL HEALTH

Plants need soil, but soil is not just a matrix which supports them; much more is going on under our feet than meets the eye. The soil ecosystem itself has been called a life support system – made up of air, water, minerals, plants, animals and microbes all of which interact and work together. This dynamic system contains a wide range of soil creatures and microbes, all contributing to the maintenance and improvement of soil health and structure.

This ecosystem that exists in the soil is delicately balanced, as with many others in the world. We cannot expect it to survive and thrive if it is physically disrupted, exploited and depleted of its essential components. Many of our research projects have looked at ways we can address these problems to support soil health while maintaining farm productivity and profitability.

At the Allerton Project, we have been involved in many studies looking at the links between crop production, soil health and water quality over the past fifteen years. Most of this research is done in collaboration with others across the UK, often involving partners and study sites in other parts of Europe. The projects we have worked on are represented on page 12, and summarised in more detail in section 6, at the end of the book.

What are the challenges to soil and water from farming?
The main challenges addressed in this document are as follows:

- Soil health – including compaction, biology and loss of organic matter
- Soil erosion – how it happens and how we can reduce it
- Sediment – the effects of soil in waterways
- Nutrient pollution

Many of these are linked; for example soil erosion leads to more sediment, and much of the phosphorus carried into surface waters when rivers are high is bound to sediment particles. Each will be discussed in its own section below.

"Healthy" soil – what does that mean?
Healthy soil has a complex mix of soil particles, minerals, microorganisms such as bacteria and fungi, organic matter, nutrients, mesofauna (small invertebrates), and larger animals such as earthworms. Together these organisms contribute to maintaining soil health, the movement and retention of nutrients and plant growth. Soil health can be defined as "the continued capacity of soil to function as a vital living ecosystem that sustains plants, animals, and humans"[7]. Soil supports life, but it must be healthy in itself to be able to continue in this role.

Is our soil healthy?
Unfortunately, large areas of soil in the UK are degraded. A study from 2015 calculated that erosion already affects around 17% of arable soils in England and Wales, with 40% at risk of erosion. It also estimated that 40% of agricultural land is liable to compaction, and that the costs of soil erosion, for example loss of crop yield, reduced carbon storage and drinking water quality, run to £1.2 billion per year in England and Wales alone[8]. Worldwide, almost two billion hectares of land are affected by human-induced soil degradation[9].

Why is this important?
Degraded soil is less able to support life – either plants above ground, or the ecosystems that should exist within soil. Healthy soil also represents a very large store of carbon[10] – the top 30cm alone is thought to contain more than twice as much carbon as is found as carbon dioxide in the atmosphere[2]. When soil becomes degraded, more of this carbon is released into the air, rather than being locked away in the ground[11]. Carbon storage is a critical component of combating climate change, and healthy soil may have an important role, alongside other approaches[12]. The 2015 Convention on Climate Change in Paris agreed an initiative to increase soil carbon by 0.4% per year, to help reduce carbon emissions and tackle climate change[13].

Does soil health affect food production?
Yes. It is thought to be a major factor limiting crop yield over the past decade or so. As well as soil being lost through erosion, growing crops in compacted soils with low organic matter limits rooting, nutrient uptake and access to water. In winter, poor quality soils are more prone to waterlogging, and crops on them are more susceptible to pests and competition from some weeds.

Is soil health regulated?
No. We rely on individual landowners to prioritise the health of their soil. Our knowledge of soil health is improving, and as we learn more we can help farmers to use sustainable techniques, which will benefit them as their soils improve. The EU drafted a framework to guide soil health, but it was not adopted by all countries. The GWCT have drafted proposals for UK agricultural policy after Brexit, which include soil measures to help improve soil health country-wide.

How do we know if soil is healthy?
We can measure soil bacteria, earthworms, organic matter and other characteristics of the soil, such as its structure, to tell us whether it is in good condition. Healthy soils are among the most diverse habitats on earth, with billions of individuals, and up to a million species of

bacteria alone living in each gram[14,15].

What do soil microbes do?

Soil microbes play a critical role in the health of soils and the plants they support. They are involved in the provision and recycling of nutrients, for example certain bacteria fix nitrogen from the atmosphere and make it accessible for plants to use. Their role in cycling nutrients means that they have a great impact on the diversity and productivity of plants[16].

What can keep soil healthy?

Traditionally, crop rotations and leaving land fallow were the approaches that maintained soil health, with what were called "exploitative" phases, when crops were grown, and "restorative" phases, when the soil was allowed to recover. However, modern methods have been developed that do not need these cycles – fertilisers and other treatments can give high yields without those rest periods, at least in the medium term.

What effect has this had?

Research suggests that soil quality is falling with continuous agriculture. Increasingly it is thought that, for food production to be sustainable in the long term, we need to adjust agricultural techniques. One approach that may help us meet the goal of sustainable agriculture is called Conservation Agriculture, which combines several of the techniques discussed in this book (see section 3.1)[17].

What is soil structure?

Soil structure describes the arrangement of the soil particles themselves, and the spaces between them. It is determined by how soil particles clump and bind together, and gives the pattern of soil pores. Soil structure is very important for water and air movement, biological activity, root growth and seedling emergence.

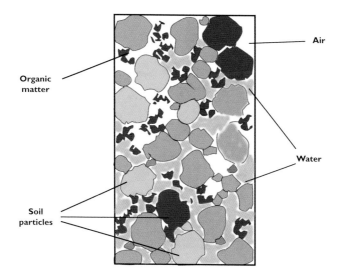

The combination of solids, water and air is critical for not only plant growth, but also surface strength. © GWCT

How can we help preserve soil structure?

Natural soil structure is disrupted by ploughing, so reducing or avoiding ploughing altogether helps preserve structure. Cover crops can be beneficial for soil structure, as can adding more organic matter to the soil.

What is organic matter?

"Organic matter" comes from living plants and creatures, so "Soil Organic Matter" is that part of the soil that is made up of dead or decaying plants or animals and dead or live microorganisms such as bacteria and fungi. Compost is organic matter, and is often used to improve garden soils.

Is it important?

Extremely. Organic matter is key for the storage of nutrients and improves fertility, as well as helping with aeration and good structure. Organic matter also affects the speed with which water filters through the soil, and increases the amount of water it can store[18]. For every 1% increase in organic matter, the soil can hold over 200,000 more litres of water per hectare[19].

How much should there be?
Different soils have very different amounts of organic matter – for example, peat is almost entirely organic. For good crop growth as well as good soil function, a guide is around 4-5% organic matter, but this does depend on soil type.

How much is there?
In baseline monitoring around the Allerton Project as part of the Water Friendly Farming study (discussed in section 3.2), soil organic matter varied between a low value of 2% and a healthy value of 5%, but with most at the lower end of the range.

What can we do to increase organic matter?
Incorporate more! For example, cover crops that are returned to the soil in the spring can help, as can including a grass phase in the rotation, as well as adding organic material such as livestock manure, slurry, or the bio-fertiliser that can be produced from biodegradable processing of green waste (biodigestate).

What reduces organic matter?
Continuous cultivation without enough time for the soil to recover between phases can reduce organic matter, as can removing crop residues such as cereal straw rather than allowing them to return to the soil. Where crop residues are removed as fodder or bedding for livestock, returning manure to the field will compensate. Ploughing can also reduce the soil's organic matter content.

Why does ploughing reduce organic matter?
Turning the soil over brings organic material from underground up and into contact with the air, which allows it to break down

more quickly[20]. This means not only that organic matter is lost from the soil faster, but also more carbon is released into the air, rather than being stored in the soil.

Don't we need to plough for farming?

Not necessarily. Non-inversion tillage avoids or reduces ploughing. The combination of very shallow cultivation and cover or mulching with crop residue helps to add organic matter to the upper soil layers. It improves soil structure and workability, reduces erosion and leaching, improves water holding capacity and creates good conditions for beneficial insects, fungi and earthworms (discussed in section 2.1).

Are earthworms important for soil?

Yes, worms eat their own weight in organic material, soil and minerals every day, making compost which enriches the soil. Where soils are healthy, there can be a greater weight of earthworms living below ground than the livestock grazing above ground. Fields that have earthworm tunnels can absorb water four to ten times faster than fields without worm tunnels, which may be important for flood management. The benefits they can bring to the farmer are shown by the finding that, in farming systems with moderate nitrogen fertiliser use, where there is a healthy earthworm population (more than 400 per square metre), there is an increase in yields, compared areas without a healthy earthworm population[21].

And ploughing affects earthworms?

Yes. Traditional ploughing turns the soil and its inhabitants upside down, and this can greatly reduce earthworm numbers by damaging the worms themselves, destroying their tunnels and making them more vulnerable to predation. The impact on earthworm populations depends on which cultivation system is used; less intense soil disturbance is less harmful for earthworms[22,23].

Where soils are healthy, there can be a greater weight of earthworms living below ground than the livestock grazing above ground. © *GWCT*

Does reducing cultivation always help?

Ploughing can disrupt the soil structure, reduce soil microbes and other animals such as earthworms, increase soil erosion and cause loss of organic matter and nutrients. It is costly in labour, time, energy and machinery. Cultivating with discs or tines, or drilling directly into stubble can allow soil to recover its structure and organic content and improve its function as an ecosystem. However, not all soil and crops are suited to reduced or no-till farming – it is important to assess local conditions, for example reduced tillage or direct drilling is harder to implement on clay soils. Ploughing can be a useful tool where black-grass is a problem, because burying the seeds when the plough turns the soil helps prevent it germinating. Reduced tillage and direct drilling are discussed further in section 2.1.

For more guidance on reduced tillage or direct drilling, please see our website: *www.gwct.org.uk/soilandwater*

What else can affect soil structure?

Compaction is another common problem on many agricultural soils. Using heavy machinery, or over stocking with livestock, can squash the soil's air pores and spaces until the soil becomes packed hard into a dense layer[24].

What effect does compaction have on soil health?

When soil is compacted it loses some or all of its ability to absorb water and air. This means that more water runs off its surface, it can be more prone to erosion and crops may not be able to grow as well because their roots cannot break through the hard-packed soil. Compaction can happen at the surface, or deeper underground below the level of the plough. Surface compaction can be remedied fairly easily, but deeper, subsoil compaction can be a difficult issue to address once it has happened[18].

1.2 SOIL EROSION

Soil erosion is a natural process, which occurs to some extent even in environments that are free of human influence. Soil particles are mobilised by water and wind, and these processes have shaped the world around us for millennia. However, man's activities have accelerated the process enormously, to the extent that soil loss and its deposition elsewhere are a real problem in many areas of the world. Most soil erosion on UK farmland happens through being washed away by water, into water courses such as streams and rivers.

How much of a problem is soil erosion?
Erosion rates differ widely across the country – depending on the landscape, soil type and land management. In some areas, it is a big problem. The amount of suspended sediment in surface runoff

water in the UK can be as much as eight grams per litre[25]. This is around one and a half teaspoons in each litre of water. Given the large amounts of water that can pass through a field each winter, a lot of soil can be washed away.

Is erosion a problem for the farm?

Yes. Soil is an essential, and non-replaceable resource. The loss of soil from fields by erosion gradually reduces the depth of topsoil remaining, and this process reduces soil productivity. The on-farm effects of soil erosion in the UK are:

- Loss of soil fertility: fertility and productivity of eroded land are reduced. More fertiliser is needed to compensate for yield losses.
- Changes in crop yields: water erosion typically affects crop production through a decrease in plant rooting depth, as well as a removal of plant nutrients and organic matter.
- Water erosion can lead to uprooting of plants and/or trees locally, together with dissection of the terrain by rills and gullies[26].

Is erosion a problem away from the farm?

Yes. Although soil loss can be serious for farms, the effects of erosion are often more severe at the site where the soil is deposited, rather than the site it is eroded from.

What can the off-site effects be?

The downstream effects can include: mud deposits after flood events, ecological damage in rivers and the need for dredging drainage channels to reduce flood risk, as well as wider impacts such as loss of carbon storage. The fact that the heaviest impacts of erosion are often felt in other locations is one reason that this problem is not being prioritised.

How much soil is eroded?

In 2000, the Soil Survey and Land Research Centre estimated that around 2.2 million tonnes of arable topsoil are eroded by water each year in the UK[1]. Other estimates range up to 2.9 million tonnes per year[27]. Across the UK, erosion estimates range from less than a tonne per hectare per year for most agricultural fields, to over twenty tonnes per hectare per year[28]. The rate is different in different places depending on land use and soil type, but in our Water Friendly Farming study area, we estimate that around half a tonne of soil is lost per hectare, per year[29].

Can erosion be reduced?

Yes. Techniques to reduce erosion are well established – in a review from 2011 it was stated that "management practices to control or decrease erosion are well documented and demonstrated to be effective – yet they are frequently not applied. Although methods suited to local conditions are still being developed, it is the adoption of erosion control methods rather than their availability that is lacking."[2]. A wide variety of erosion mitigation measures are available and have been studied, many of which can show real benefits. However, their effectiveness is highly dependent on local circumstances – for example soil type, slope, climate and crop[28]. The mitigation measures we have studied at the Allerton Project will be explored in more detail in section 2.

1.3 SEDIMENT

Sediment is soil that is washed from the fields into watercourses. It carries other things with it, such as nutrients and chemicals, but is also a pollutant in its own right, reducing the available light and oxygen levels. When sediment is high in streams and rivers it can settle out when the water flow slows downstream, and be deposited as silt on the bottom of the watercourse. Not only is this a loss for the field, it can be harmful for the stream, river or lake it ends up in.

How does eroded soil get into waterways?
There are two main routes for soil to get into water courses – surface runoff, where the water runs over the ground and into ditches or streams, or sub-surface flow, normally from field drains, which also run into ditches or streams[25].

How much sediment travels via field drains compared to surface runoff?

There are not many studies looking at this, but it seems that, although surface runoff usually has a higher sediment concentration, much more water travels through the field drain network, meaning that most sediment actually comes through field drains. It is more dilute and has a smaller particle size, but there is a lot more of it. One study found that forty times more water came through field drains than surface runoff, carrying twenty times as much sediment overall[25].

Can sediment cause problems when it gets into waterways?

Yes. High levels of sediment can make rivers cloudy, which reduces the amount of light that enters the water, and how far it can penetrate. This can affect the plants and animals that live there, and change the ecosystem[28,31].

Field Drains

There are several kinds of field drains, which are buried, at various depths usually between around 0.75m and 1.5m under the surface, depending on the soil type and landscape[30]. They can be clay or plastic pipes, with holes pierced along them to allow water to enter, they can be gravel filled, or they can simply be tunnels through the soil itself ('mole drains'). A network of field drains connects underground to cover the whole field, and discharges water into a ditch or stream at the bottom of a field[30].

It is thought that around 40% of lowland agricultural areas in the UK are under-drained in some way[25]. Field drains are used more on heavy clay soils, in arable areas. All the arable fields at Loddington, and in our Water Friendly Farming project study area, are under-drained.

How does sediment affect river ecosystems?
High levels of sediment in rivers can be harmful to aquatic invertebrates. These are small creatures that live in water such as insects, plankton, the larvae of many different species, worms and water snails. Invertebrates are critical as the building blocks of the ecosystem – they provide the food for many larger animals as well as consuming debris such as leaves. It is well known that they are affected by increased sediment, for example, many are filter feeders and their feeding structures can become clogged up with sediment so they cannot feed efficiently[32]. Lots of invertebrate species live on the bottom of river beds, and can become buried by deposits of sediment and algae (which is increased by the extra nutrients transported to the river by sediment).

What effect can sediment have on fish?
Sediment deposits on the gravel beds of rivers can clog and compact the gravel that fish spawn in. Fine silt particles can smother fish eggs, reduce water flow through the gravel bed and reduce the available oxygen[33]. Sediment also reduces the available spaces between gravel and cobbles, which young fish use to save energy by keeping out of the main river flow, as well as to hide from predators.

What effect does this have?
Breeding success for salmonids (the fish family that includes salmon and trout) is lower in spawning sites with high levels of fine sediment. This is for two reasons; firstly sediment can block the spaces between gravel where eggs are laid, and interrupt the water flow over the eggs, which reduces their oxygen supply. Secondly, depending on the organic content of the sediment, the sediment itself can use oxygen from the water, which further reduces its availability to eggs[33-36].

Does this have an effect on the overall population?
It is generally accepted that increased levels of fine sediment in rivers has impacted breeding success, early mortality and many

other aspects of biology and behaviour for some fish species[33]. For example, for those that feed by sight, foraging for food is harder in a murky river. We know that sediment contributes to poor egg survival, but because of the complex interaction of lots of factors, it has not been conclusively shown that sediment has reduced salmonid populations overall.

River Frome Salmon numbers

Average 1973-1990 = 1897

Average 1973-1990 = 830

The long-term annual data on adult salmon numbers 1973-2016. Visit www.gwct.org.uk/fishing for more information.

What can we do to help?
In this situation, prevention is certainly better than cure. Reducing soil erosion from agricultural soils is much easier than cleaning up rivers. Some farming practices, for example allowing livestock direct access to river banks, have been shown to increase erosion. GWCT research has shown that fencing river banks in areas with predominantly livestock farming can reduce erosion and increase river bank vegetation[36,37].

Can we clean up silted streams?

Gravel cleaning is a technique used by some to remove sediment that has already settled on the gravel bed. It can improve the local conditions for spawning[38], at the cost of a temporary reduction in some other aquatic species[36]. If the original cause of the sedimentation is an ongoing problem, the river bed will likely silt up again over time.

How is gravel cleaning done?

The most effective way of gravel cleaning uses a high pressure hose to spray a jet of water into the river bed, which disturbs the sediment, allowing it to wash downstream.

Does this help?

It can help locally, removing sediment enough for salmonid egg survival to be higher in the two years afterwards, but the river gradually silts up again, and survival drops by the third year[39]. The need for gravel to be cleaned is a sign that there is an underlying problem with erosion and sediment. Although gravel washing can help temporarily, it is not a substitute for reducing erosion in the long term.

What other effects are caused by sediment?

Silting in rivers and lakes can cause economic problems as well as ecological ones. It can also disrupt river flow, with consequences for flooding, and the river must be dredged. When high levels of sediment are found in streams this also shows that agricultural soil erosion is happening, which reduces both farm productivity and the water storage capacity of the landscape. The amount of water held in reservoirs for drinking water supply can also be reduced by sediment deposits, and sediment can transport other pollutants to the water[3].

What other pollutants can it carry?

Sediment can carry many things into the water course with it, including toxic metals, pathogens, nutrients, veterinary medicines and some pesticides, for example the weed killers propyzamide and glyphosate, and the active ingredient of some slug pellets, metaldehyde[28].

What effects can nutrients have?

Nutrients can have a large effect on surface waters, with high levels causing excess growth of aquatic plants. This may lead to toxic algal blooms, deoxygenation of water, and fish deaths[40]. This is discussed in section 2.4.

The images above show the condition of the Trenant Brook before and after gravel washing in 2017 © GWCT

Where does most sediment come from?
There are many sources of sediment across the countryside, but it is thought that up to 75% of the total amount of sediment carried into surface waters courses comes from agriculture[11,41]. Perhaps this is to be expected, as 75% of the UK is farmland, but it is important to identify the sources, and try to reduce this movement of soil from fields to rivers. Both because farmers need the soil on their fields, and because sediment can cause damage elsewhere.

This satellite photograph of Great Britain shows soil escaping our rivers and into the sea.
© NERC Satellite Receiving Station, Dundee University, Scotland www.sat.dundee.ac.uk

1.4 NUTRIENT CONTAMINATION OF WATER

Although we tend to think of nutrients as being beneficial, they are naturally found at fairly low levels in fresh water. Human activities, like adding fertiliser to soil, can raise these levels. This process is called "eutrophication". It can be harmful to fish and other aquatic creatures, and is one of many forms of pollution.

When nutrient levels are raised, ponds and lakes can become choked with algae or blanket weed which smothers the natural species.

Which nutrients can cause these problems?
Nitrogen and phosphorus are the main nutrients we are concerned by, both because of drinking water contamination (which is covered by the Nitrates Directive) and the excessive growth of plant life they can cause - which can dramatically disrupt the ecosystem.

What does this mean?

Just as adding nutrients to the soil helps plants to grow on land, increased levels of nutrients in the water can allow increased plant growth, or excessive algae growth. Water can become cloudy from the algae, and sunlight cannot reach submerged plants. When plants and algae then die and decompose, the decomposition process uses oxygen from the water, reducing the oxygen available for other species. Without enough dissolved oxygen in the water, fish and other organisms can't survive. This disrupts the normal balance, and can lead to changes such as algal blooms and acidification of the water, where other species suffer. This process can occur locally, or much further downstream leading to degraded estuaries, lakes and reservoirs.

How does phosphorus get into the water system?

Phosphorus comes mainly from fertiliser, manure and sewage. Phosphorus is a useful example of the close link between soil and water management, as one of its forms – phosphates – binds very tightly to soil particles, and is therefore mainly transported to water courses by erosion.

What forms are there?

Phosphorus is usually thought of in two categories – that which is bound to sediment particles, particulate phosphorus, and that which is dissolved in the water itself. The soluble forms tend to be more "bioavailable", meaning that plants can access it, and use it. This type of available phosphorus may have more impact than the phosphorus that is carried with the sediment from fields. For example, phosphorus can get into water from sewage treatment plants, septic tanks, and farmyards or animal manure, and this tends to be in a much more bioavailable form than particulate phosphorus. This is an important area of research that is ongoing.

Has this been researched by the Allerton Project?

Yes, the Allerton Project was part of a collaboration looking at phosphorus in the streams that run through farmland. Along with sites in Hereford and Hampshire, the river Welland was extensively studied in the five-year Defra funded PARIS study (Phosphorus from Agriculture: Riverine Impacts Study)[5,42].

What did PARIS find?

PARIS showed that in terms of the total amount of phosphorus of all forms across the year in the study catchments, agriculture was the main source, being responsible for 67-99%[42]. However, other sources were also important. For example, phosphorus coming from farmland is highest in winter – when storms wash sediment and phosphorus from fields. Other sources such as domestic septic tanks, waste water from buildings, animal waste from farmyards and sewage works (called "point" sources) discharge phosphorus more steadily throughout the year, even though the total annual amount is lower[5,42,43].

Is this important?

It is very important, because during the spring, summer and early autumn, when ecosystems are more sensitive to nutrient changes, most phosphorus is coming from domestic sources. In fact, they are the main source of phosphorus for more of the year than farmed land. This is an important discovery of our research.

What sort of phosphorus comes from these sources?

Most phosphorus from animal and human waste is in a dissolved, bioavailable form – approximately 90% of the phosphorus in septic tank effluent entering streams was bioavailable in the PARIS project[43]. The phosphorus coming from farmland was found to be 10-20% bioavailable, with most of it particulate bound[43].

Does this mean that we shouldn't worry about phosphorus attached to sediment?
No. It is important, but the picture is very complex. Sediment itself can be harmful. We need the soil to remain on the fields, and when eroded it can carry other substances that we should strive to keep out of rivers. The PARIS project concentrated on streams, where water flows quickly. Further downstream, larger rivers flow more slowly and sediment may be even more likely to settle out, so it is possible that the effect of sediment and phosphorus from farmland may in fact be felt more keenly further away.

Does it mean that phosphorus from farming is not important?
No, not at all. For example, PARIS also showed that livestock farming on clay soils near to water courses can lead to the highest phosphorus concentrations. It is important to reduce pollution from farmland as far as possible, but it is also important to recognise other sources that might be damaging and reduce these as well[43].

What can be done about point sources?
Many septic tanks are old, not well maintained, and emptied too infrequently, therefore releasing more pollution than they should6. A report to Natural England in 2010 found that 80% of septic tanks are probably working inefficiently[6]. Each individual one may not contribute very much, but overall their contribution to pollution is likely to be much larger than we had realised. For large settlements, sewage treatment works have improved in recent years with respect to nutrient losses, although more can be done, and in small rural settlements, phosphorus discharges can be substantial[29].

What about nitrogen?
Nitrogen is often added to soil in the form of fertilisers to help crops grow in the spring or summer, but any excess which remains can later be leached away to water courses when the heavier rains of winter fall on bare soil. Farming is the main source of nitrogen pollution in waterways, and efforts should be made to reduce

nitrogen discharge. Much of England has have been designated as "Nitrate Vulnerable Zones" (NVZs), with the aim of reducing nitrate loss from agriculture.

Does all nutrient pollution come from farming?
No, but it is a major source. Agriculture is thought to contribute 70% of the nitrogen and 28% of the phosphorus load to UK waters[3].

How widespread a problem is nitrogen pollution?
It had long been thought that nitrogen was less of a concern than phosphorus in water bodies, however evidence now suggests that it is more important than we realised. Despite a long-term, gradual decrease in stream nitrogen concentrations, nitrogen is still more widely present than phosphorus in water bodies. Up to 95% of water bodies in the UK have raised levels of nitrogen and most streams in agricultural areas have nitrogen levels high enough to be considered ecologically damaging, even though they may be below the drinking water limit[4,43].

What is a Nitrate Vulnerable Zone?
An area where nitrate might exceed the limit set for water, which is 50mg per litre. This can be for groundwater, surface water or where bodies of water may become eutrophic.

Why is the limit set at 50mg/l?
The evidence for the limit is not clear, and several groups have expressed concerns about this. Natural England suggested to an investigation by the House of Commons Environmental, Food and Rural Affairs Committee in 2008 that the limit had no ecological relevance.

How does being in an NVZ affect farming?
To try and reduce nitrate pollution, there are extra rules about how farmers can use and store nitrogen-based fertilisers, manures, slurry etc. Farmers must produce a plan of fertiliser use, and keep their usage of nitrogen within strict limits. They need to consider the

risks of run-off contaminating water, how much nitrogen their crops need, how much is in the soil and how much will be added in the fertiliser/manure/slurry. There are strict restrictions about where nitrogen cannot be added – for example, within 2 metres of a water course or established hedge, as well as periods in the year when different kinds of fertiliser must not be spread. Detailed records must be kept of all nitrogen use for 5 years, and may be inspected.

What governs water quality in the UK?
The EU's Water Framework Directive (WFD) currently governs much of the work in managing and protecting our rivers, lakes, coastal waters and estuaries.

What does the Water Framework Directive say?
The WFD was introduced in 2000, and aimed for all surface and ground water to be in "good" chemical and ecological condition by 2015. It provides a framework for all EU countries to improve water quality, and although this aim was not achieved by 2015, the WFD and other measures such as the Groundwater Directive and the Nitrate Directive are thought to have had a positive impact on water across the EU[44].

Is UK water clean?
Most water bodies in lowland UK have raised levels of phosphorus, nitrogen or both, but pockets of clean water do remain. Baseline measurements taken by the Freshwater Habitats Trust at the beginning of our Water Friendly Farming project (described in section 3.2) showed that on average only 7% of water bodies would be thought of as "clean" in terms of nutrients[4]. This project was carried out in a lowland agricultural landscape in Leicestershire, typical of large areas of the country. This highlights the work that needs to be done in such environments, but a higher fraction of water bodies are still clean in other areas of the UK, particularly those less affected by farming, effluents from sewage works and runoff from urban areas.

Most water bodies in the UK have raised levels of phosphorus, nitrogen or both, but pockets of clean water do remain. © GWCT

2. Finding solutions

Problems with soil health, soil function, and water quality are widespread, and it is imperative that we do our best to reduce the effects we are having on these essential resources. Many approaches have been suggested and trialled, and we concentrate here on those that we have studied at the GWCT's Allerton Project.

Reduced tillage can reduce erosion, particularly where soils are prone to it. © GWCT

43

© GWCT

2.1 REDUCED OR NO-TILL FARMING

Used to:
- Reduce crop establishment costs
- Reduce erosion
- Improve soil structure
- Increase organic matter
- Retain nutrients

What is reduced or no-tillage?
Tillage is preparing the ground for growing crops, and is traditionally done with a plough. Conservation tillage uses either no ploughing, with direct planting of seeds into the residue from the previous crop, or non-inversion (reduced) cultivation where ground is not turned over, and preparation is kept to a minimum. The surface can be scratched with tines or discs, rather than turning over with a

traditional plough.

What does tillage do?
Tillage prepares the ground for sowing seed, by breaking up the soil and turning it over. This provides a clean, fine tilth for sowing into. Turning over with the plough also buries the seeds of some weed species, making it harder for them to germinate which helps with weed control. It gives the crops an edge over the weeds in the competition for growth.

Why do we not want to do these things?
Turning over the soil also comes with disadvantages: it can damage soil structure, expose the soil to erosion, reduce organic matter in soil, and reduce the number of earthworms, other soil creatures and microbes[20,45–48]. Although ploughing is often helpful to the farmer in the short term, these things that are damaged by ploughing are important for healthy functioning of the soil in the long term.

Why is this important?
Sustainability in farming is becoming more and more important. Many soils are gradually degrading after decades of cultivation, and this is having an impact not only on farming but also on the environment more widely. Looking after our soils, and therefore our water quality and water courses, is an essential part of farming for the future.

Can reduced or no-tillage help?
Many studies have looked at reduced or no-till farming across the world in recent decades, and many advantages have been shown including; increased earthworm abundance, improved soil structure, reduced erosion, lower nutrient losses and reduced crop establishment costs[2,20,47,49–52].

What effect does this have on the farming system?
No-till is a different approach, that will take some time to adjust

to. For example, drilling directly into crop residue is not as easy as drilling into a ploughed field, conditions need to be right, and machinery may need to be adjusted accordingly. As ploughing can help control some weeds, weed pressure can be higher in the transition period to no-till farming, with an increased reliance on herbicides for control. However, no-till brings many benefits that can offset these challenges.

Are yields affected?
For some crops, yields are lower initially with reduced tillage. Reduced tillage is also not suitable for all soil types and climates – it tends to be more beneficial on sandy or loamy soils than clay. However, a large study looking at the effect of tillage on yields across Europe concluded that, because costs were lower (mostly because of lower fuel bills and labour costs), reduced tillage was on average more profitable despite reduced yields for maize and winter crops. Reduced tillage gave 4.5% lower yields, and no-till 8.5% lower[53].

Has reduced tillage been studied by the Allerton Project?
Yes. the Allerton Project was involved in a large international research project called the SOil and WAter Protection project (SOWAP), which set out to compare the traditional ploughing approach to conservation tillage (CT). Conservation tillage is the minimum soil disturbance required to establish a crop, and can refer to a range of different techniques but in most cases discs or tines were used to cultivate the soil before planting.

What did SOWAP look at?
SOWAP looked at the environmental impacts of conservation tillage on a broad scale, including soil quality, soil microbes, earthworms, soil porosity, erosion and water quality, as well as crop yields and overall economic performance.

What did SOWAP find?
SOWAP clearly showed that reduced tillage can reduce erosion,

particularly where soils are prone to it. On some reduced tillage plots, surface runoff was lower by 90%, and on some sites that were prone to it, erosion dropped by up to 95%[49].

In general, reduced tillage also reduced water runoff, soil erosion, loss of nutrients and carbon loss from the majority of plots in which it was implemented. It was also shown to decrease nitrogen losses, and in some cases phosphorus losses, but this was not as consistent[18,49,58].

Higher levels of soil nitrogen were found on reduced tillage plots than conventional tillage plots, perhaps because nitrogen is held in the soil better, rather than being washed away. The results were heavily influenced by soil type, with reduced tillage being more beneficial on lighter, sandier soils. An increase in organic carbon content, and increased soil moisture content in reduced tillage soils were also shown[49,58]. Reduced tillage created a better environment for earthworms than conventional ploughing[18].

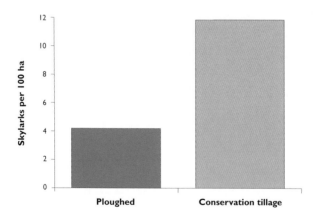

Average number of skylarks seen per visit to UK winter crops cultivated with conventional ploughing or conservation tillage during January-March. Birds were surveyed monthly, over a three year period, on between seven and nine farms. From Conservation Agriculture in Europe. SOWAP. 2006[18], adapted from Cunningham et al, 2005[59]. © GWCT

The increased ground cover caused by reduced tillage provided an extended nesting period for skylarks © David Mason

What effect does reduced tillage have for biodiversity?

SOWAP studied the effect of reduced tillage on biodiversity and found many benefits[18], including:

- Increased ground cover was helpful for ground-nesting birds. For example, extending the nesting period for skylarks[54]
- More diversity in cropping gave a wider range of feeding and nesting opportunities for birds[18]
- More weed seeds and grain were left on the soil surface, which can help feed animals in winter[55]
- Ploughing reduces the number of earthworms in the soil, so not ploughing allowed them to recover and increase[56]
- A wider range and abundance of soil microbes compared to conventional tillage[57]
- Reduced sediment and nutrient loads entering water courses was better for aquatic life[58]

Is reduced tillage widely practiced?

The amount of land that is traditionally ploughed is gradually falling. In Europe as a whole, about 15% of arable land is thought to be under conservation tillage, with less than 1% in no-till and 14% minimally tilled (where non-inversion tillage is carried out with discs or tines). In the UK this is higher: in 2006 almost half of all arable land was under conservation tillage, and 3% under no-till[18]. It has been adopted more rapidly and more widely in the Americas than in Europe, but it seems to be rising across the world.

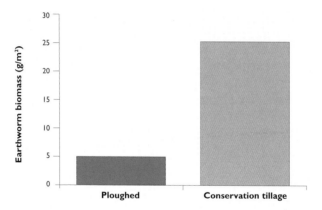

Average earthworm biomass from plots either ploughed or under conservation tillage in Hungary. From Conservation Agriculture in Europe. SOWAP. 2006[18]

2.2 COVER CROPS

Used to:
- Reduce erosion
- Improve soil structure
- Retain nutrients
- Increase organic matter

What are cover crops?

Cover crops are planted to protect the soil between the harvest of one crop and planting of the next, when the soil would otherwise be left fallow or bare. This can either be for a short period in summer (around 2 months), or 6-8 months over the autumn/winter prior to a spring crop[60].

Why are cover crops used?

Cover crops can protect the soil, reduce erosion from wind and water, improve soil structure and take up nutrients, reducing their leaching from the soil[61–63]. Our own research at the Allerton Project shows that some cover crop species can suppress weeds in winter, and carry this benefit through to reduce weeds in the following crop[60].

How do cover crops affect nutrient loss?

Cover crops take up nutrients through the winter, capturing them and holding them within the plants. These can then be returned to the soil as "green manure" in time for the planting of crops in spring. These nutrients are then available for the spring crop just as the seeds germinate, rather than being lost from the soil to streams over the winter. This can retain nutrients, particularly nitrogen, cycling it within the field and reducing the amount which leaches away from the bare soil over winter.

How do they reduce erosion?

Cover crops give a protective layer over the soil, rather than leaving it bare. This absorbs some of the force that rain drops have when they hit the surface (rain splash erosion), and shelters the soil. Cover crops are also thought to improve soil structure, which makes soil more resistant to erosion.

Has the Allerton Project looked at cover crops?

Yes. As part of the Sustainable Intensification research Platform (SIP), we were part of a series of Defra studies aiming to identify and develop farm management techniques to help improve the sustainability of agriculture[63].

What did we study?

At the Allerton Project, we compared different species of cover crops to each other, and to bare stubble, for their effect on soil health, earthworms, weed burden over winter, and weed burden and yield in the following crop. The soils at the Allerton Project are a heavy clay, where the benefits of cover crops are thought to be smaller than on other soils.

What did it show?
It showed that cover crops could be used over winter without harming the following crop, and in fact some species of cover crops can benefit the crop that is grown afterwards[60].

How do they help?
Fields planted with certain species of cover crops had fewer weeds in winter and there were fewer weeds and a higher yield in the spring-sown crop that followed. They can also have subtle effects on soil chemistry, biology and structure; for example some crops had increased earthworm numbers[60].

How do cover crops suppress weeds?
They compete for the same resources that weeds need. For example, when the cover crop has germinated and is providing ground cover, it is also blocking some of the light that weed seedlings would otherwise be able to use.

Do all cover crops have these effects?
No, it is important to choose the species carefully so that it suits your environment, soil type and aims. On the clay soil at Allerton, the SIP showed that a cover crop mix of 4:1 oats to radish reduced the number of weeds over winter, that earthworms increased with radish cover crops, and phospohorus levels increased with phacelia or vetch[60,63].

What species are used for cover crops?
A range of species can be used, including legumes (peas, beans etc), cereals and brassicas. Different species perform different roles, including capturing nitrogen from the atmosphere, capturing and mobilising phosphorus and improving soil physical structure. They have different rooting structures, grow at different rates and

so on, so the choice of species depends on the task that is required. A mix can be more beneficial than a single species, for example, oat, radish and phacelia.

Are cover crops always helpful?
Not necessarily, it depends what the farmer wants to use them for. The benefits can also be different on different soil types – for example, on clay soils there is usually a less pronounced effect. A good knowledge of how and when to use cover crops and which species to plant is essential to make best use of the benefits they can give. Cover crops are a fairly recent addition to the farming toolkit, and many farmers have reported possible benefits of incorporating them. Some of these are confirmed by scientific research and others are still under investigation, but overall it seems that cover crops may have much to offer in the right conditions.

Are there drawbacks to using cover crops?
Cover crops can slow the warming of the soil in spring, as they shade the surface from the sun. Also, there are costs associated with buying and drilling the seed. Where managed correctly, in the right conditions, these are usually offset by the benefits, but this highlights why increased knowledge and planning is required when adopting a new technique.

2.3 TRAMLINE MANAGEMENT

Used to:
- Reduce runoff
- Reduce erosion
- Reduce nutrient loss

How can we help to reduce surface runoff?
One of the studies the Allerton Project has been involved in was called MOPS – Mitigation Options for Phosphorus and Sediment. One of the many important findings was that most of the soil being carried away over the surface of a field comes from the tramlines[64].

Why do tramlines contribute to soil erosion?
They provide an easy route for surface water to run along, carrying with it eroded soil, rather than the water soaking into the surface.

In the MOPS project, significantly more water, sediment and phosphorus ran off areas of a field with tramlines, compared to areas without. Across the three farms that were part of the project, there was between two and 200 times more sediment coming from study plots with tramlines, than from plots without. At the Allerton Project, runoff from tramline plots was three times higher than that from plots without tramlines[64], and 80% of sediment came from areas of the field with tramlines[65].

© GWCT

Tramlines

Tramlines are the compacted, unseeded tyre tracks that tractors drive along in fields. They act as a guide for farmers to ensure that the whole crop is evenly and efficiently treated, whilst minimizing crop damage from tractor wheels.

What can we do to reduce this?
MOPS tested different ways to reduce surface runoff and erosion, and found several options, with the best depending on the location of the farm and field.

Contour cultivation, which means planting and managing your fields across the slope rather than up-and-down the slope, is very effective for reducing erosion, especially on clay soils with a moderate slope. If the slope is shallow enough, this change has no effect on income, but can dramatically reduce runoff and erosion (a suitable slope is less than around 5 degrees – a general guide is that at this angle, a ball does not roll down the slope). However, in most landscapes there are few suitable fields, as most fields slope in different directions and the tramlines cannot follow the slope all the way across the field. The project also found an association between beetle banks along the contour and lower rates of erosion, but this also needs to follow an even slope to be effective, and has the same problem where slopes are complex[65].

What if you can't cultivate across the slope?
If the slope is too steep, slopes in many directions, or it doesn't suit your field for other reasons, there are alternatives. At sites with sandy or silty loam soils, using tines to disrupt the surface of the soil on tramlines allowed water to soak in, and was the best way of reducing tramline runoff and erosion[64]. Reduced or no-till farming are of increasing interest for many reasons, including lower erosion and runoff than traditional cultivations as well as improved soil health and reduced nutrient loss.

Following the initial findings from MOPS, a five-year Defra funded tramlines project was started at the Allerton Project and three other sites across the UK to look at the best ways to reduce runoff, erosion and nutrient loss from tramlines.

© *GWCT*

Beetle Banks

A beetle bank is a raised strip running across the field, around 2m wide and 0.5m high, disconnected from the field edge to allow normal agricultural operations. It is planted with a range of tussocky grasses, to provide cover and shelter for wildlife. They are beneficial for integrated pest control, allowing pest eating insects over-winter shelter away from the field edge, have advantages for biodiversity and are supported by agri-environment schemes.

What did the tramlines research study?

This study focussed on how to adjust practices for autumn spraying. Driving along tramlines at this time of year, when soils are wet and easy to compact, can contribute the most to runoff, soil erosion and phosphate losses. The tramlines study looked at and compared tramlines from conventional tyres with:

1. **Low pressure tyres**, inflated to around half the pressure normally used in agricultural vehicles. These spread the load and reduce compaction, making it easier for water to soak in, rather than runoff (tyres used were Michelin Agribib and Xeobib agricultural tyres).

2. A **rotary harrow** attached to the tractor to break up the surface tramlines behind the wheels after the tractor passes.

3. A **"surface profiler"**, which disrupts the soil in tramlines, and then shapes it so that the soil is raised in a curved shape behind the tractor, rather than the usual gullies that water can drain down. When water lands on this raised ridge, it should run back into the cropped area and soak in, rather than running down the tramlines and away, carrying soil with it.

4. **Drilling (planting) tramlines**, rather than leaving them bare. Autumn spraying operations were then guided with GPS, rather than following the tramlines to guide spraying.

What did it show?
Overall, options 1-3 could be effective. Drilling tramlines did not seem to help. Surface runoff can be reduced by up to 75% using low pressure tyres, 95% using a rotary harrow, and 85% using a surface profiler[66].

Were these results consistent?
Results varied at different sites because of different local conditions such as soil type, slope, rainfall etc. Results also varied year-to-year. For example, low rainfall in winter 2010/11 meant that sediment and phosphate losses were low from the clay soils at the Allerton Project, so no effect was seen from the tests that year, whereas effects were seen at the other three sites and in other years.

Which were the best?

The low-pressure tyres and rotary harrow were the most promising techniques in years one and two of the study and were examined in more detail, both separately and together, in year three (2011/12). This was a much wetter year, and results showed that both were helpful for reducing runoff, sediment and phosphorus loss, and were even more effective when used together[66].

Computer modelling was used to predict which techniques would be the most effective under different conditions. This showed that the rotary harrow is best in all scenarios except for clay soils, where the low-pressure tyres are more effective. However, both approaches are very effective, each reducing sediment loss by more than half compared to conventional techniques[66].

Are these techniques expensive?

Low pressure tyres, also called "very flexible" tyres are more expensive to buy than standard agricultural tyres, but they have a longer expected lifespan. Taking both factors into account, they can give a £2 per hectare saving on a 300-hectare farm. The rotary harrow costs around £12 per hectare if only applied to 20% of a 300-hectare farm, but these costs are likely to fall as it is becoming clear that they can also be used across other crop rotations. Some Agri-Environment schemes now have capital grants available for tramline management[66].

Is tramline management the whole answer?

Tramline management is one tool that can be used to reduce erosion and water runoff. Other options can be used in conjunction with this, for example cover crops, in-field barriers or buffer strips[64].

2.4 In-field wetlands

Used to:
- Trap sediment
- Reduce nutrient transfer to streams

What are in-field wetlands?
In-field wetlands are unlined basins, excavated either in field margins or other unproductive, naturally wet areas of the field. In a project called MOPS2, three designs were tested to see if they could reduce the sediment in water flowing off arable fields by slowing it down and allowing the sediment to settle out before the water entered the stream. Different designs were compared, including shallow wetlands, deep wetlands and some arranged in pairs. Wetlands were placed so that they could intercept water from different sources: surface runoff, field drains, ditches and streams[67].

What did MOPS2 show?

On the right soil type, in-field wetlands can effectively reduce sediment in water. The concentration of sediment in water can be up to 60% lower when it leaves a wetland than when it entered. The effectiveness of wetlands is heavily influenced by local conditions, particularly the type of soil. Wetlands work better at sandy soil sites than clay soil sites such as Loddington where very little sediment accumulated over the three years of the project[67].

Why do they work better at sandy sites?

The particles in sandy soils are larger, and can settle out more quickly. Clay soils are made up of very fine particles, which take a long time to settle out, so field wetlands are much less effective in these areas.

How much sediment can they remove?

The total amount of sediment trapped was very different between sites because of these soil type differences. However, at the Whinton Hill site, 26 tonnes of sediment was trapped by a single wetland in one year during 2009/10, which would otherwise have flowed into local watercourses[67].

Does MOPS2 agree with other research?

Yes. Defra published a thorough review of whether wetlands can reduce agricultural pollution, and concluded "The overall finding of the review was that all wetland types are very effective at reducing major nutrients and suspended sediments"[68]. Despite the finding by MOPS2 that they are less effective on clay, overall field wetlands are a useful tool to reduce sedimentation.

Do on-farm wetlands have any other role?

Farmland has become a much drier place in recent decades, so we thought that these wetlands could also be important for birds and farmland biodiversity. We set up a separate Defra-funded research project called "Wetting up Farmland for Biodiversity" to see if this is the case.

What did Wetting up Farmland for Biodiversity look at?
The project looked at different types of water feature in the farmed landscape. The effect on farmland biodiversity was recorded by counting the number of visits from birds, and the number of aquatic insects that emerged at each feature throughout the year.

What did it show?
Dammed ditches and field corner paired ponds were wet all year round, and had more visits from birds than the reference areas. A wide variety of birds visited the sites, where they were seen drinking, feeding, bathing and displaying territorial behaviours. The number of insects emerging was also higher in dammed ditches, especially those with more wet mud exposed and less shade[69].

The creation of farmland ditches and ponds resulted in an increased number of visits from many birds, including wren, tree sparrow, yellowhammer and dunnock. © Laurie Campbell/GWCT

How much do in-field wetlands cost?

It is difficult to calculate a cost for each tonne of sediment removed, because it depends on soil type, rainfall, location in the country, and location within a farm. However, the costs of making and maintaining the wetlands in this study were between £280 and £3100 - low enough to be supported through an agri-environment scheme, perhaps with capital payments for reducing sediment or phosphorus pollution to water courses. Ongoing costs of dredging, needed approximately every 4 years for dammed ditches, are estimated at £10 per ditch per year[70]. The wetlands were placed on field edges or unproductive areas, and therefore represent little loss to agricultural production[67].

The effectiveness of wetlands is heavily influenced by local conditions, particularly the type of soil. © GWCT

2.5 BUFFER STRIPS AND BARRIERS

Used to:
- Reduce sediment transfer to streams
- Reduce nutrient transfer to streams

The measures discussed above to reduce soil erosion will help to keep soil on fields, and this will therefore reduce sediment in water courses[28]. However, once soil has been eroded from fields and is suspended in water, it is still possible to intercept the transport of that sediment from the field into streams, for example with in-field barriers and field-edge buffer strips.

What are barriers and buffer strips?
An in-field barrier is a slightly raised strip along the contour of the slope, planted with vegetation. One form of these, the beetle bank, is already

funded by agri-environment schemes for the benefit of biodiversity and becoming widely used. Positioning them along contours – across the slope, rather than up and down, means they can also act as a barrier for water and sediment. They slow the flow of water, and give it more of a chance to soak into the ground, instead of running quickly over the surface. A buffer strip is a vegetated area along the lower edge of the fields and against a watercourse. These have been shown to reduce sediment and nutrient losses from surface runoff, as well as being good for biodiversity.

How wide are they?

Buffer strips along the edge of water courses must be a minimum of 2m wide to comply with "cross-compliance" regulations governing basic farming techniques. These must be adhered to in order to receive the basic farm payment. In-field barriers are generally a similar width, but are raised to create a narrow ridge around 40cm high. Modelling of Water Friendly Farming project data suggests that wider buffer strips are more effective for reducing sediment[29].

How effective are they?

Results from our work in the MOPS1 project showed that at Allerton, a beetle bank located along the field contour could reduce sediment and phosphorus by 9-97%. This is a wide range, but shows that they have the potential to be effective, at modest cost.

Do they have other benefits?

All the measures discussed above to reduce soil erosion and catch sediment will also reduce phosphorus pollution, as phosphates are carried into water courses bound to sediment[28]. These features also have important benefits for biodiversity on the farm, providing habitat for invertebrates, birds and small mammals.

Domestic impact: Septic Tank Systems

Many rural communities in the UK are not connected to main sewage systems, and the majority of these rely on septic tank systems (STS) to manage their sewage output. Many are old, and as there is no registration system for them, their design, operation and distribution are not known. In particular, soakaways are often ineffective on clay soils, leading to direct discharge to watercourses. A report to Natural England in 2010 estimated that over 80% of septic tanks in the UK are probably not working efficiently[6].

Although agriculture is often assumed to be the main source of freshwater nutrient pollution, a study carried out by the GWCT, the University of Bangor and the Centre for Ecology and Hydrology, looked at the effect of septic tanks on the streams they discharge into. This showed that septic tanks should be a real concern for water quality in rural areas. They deliver varying but generally high concentrations of potentially toxic nutrients to the stream network, especially in summer[5].

It is very important that septic tanks are installed and maintained correctly so that they function properly. The combined factors of increasing rural populations and climate change are likely to exacerbate these pressures on freshwater systems, and the impact of septic tanks may increase.

3. Bringing it together

These individual techniques which address certain areas of concern can be combined into broader farming systems which have soil health, conservation and water quality at their heart. The use of several principles together can magnify the advantages of these individual techniques and lead to greater gains on a larger scale across the countryside.

Monitoring soil quality is a vital tool in understanding the impact of different agricultural practices © GWCT

3.1 CONSERVATION AGRICULTURE

Conservation Agriculture (CA) is a combination of three principles:

- Reduced or no-tillage
- Permanent ground cover
- Crop rotation

CA is becoming increasingly more common in recent years, particularly in the Americas, but also in Europe. There are many suggested benefits of the approach, both for the farmer and for the environment. Reduced tillage was discussed in section 2.1, but the combination with two other important principles makes up the broader approach of Conservation Agriculture.

What is permanent ground cover?

Permanent ground cover is provided either by leaving crop residue (such as stubble) from the previous harvest rather than ploughing it in, or by planting green cover like cover crops for the purpose. It protects the surface of the soil in winter from erosion, as well as improving soil structure and organic matter. Crop residues provide benefits including surface protection and addition of organic matter, but cover crops can perform extra services such as capturing nitrogen.

What is a good crop rotation?

Crop rotation is the cornerstone of sustainable farming, and it means alternating the crop grown in one place, rather than growing the same crop again and again on the same land. Growing a minimum of four different crops in a cycle is usual - although more would be better. It builds soil fertility and reduces pests and diseases. Including livestock in the rotation is beneficial as it recycles nutrients and organic matter to the soil. The crops within a rotation will depend on local conditions, markets and prices, but there are some broad principles:

- Crops that build soil fertility (e.g. peas/beans/clover and grass) should be alternated with those that reduce fertility (e.g. cereals, potatoes and sugar beet).
- The sequence of crops should be used to control grass weeds in broad-leaf crops and broad-leaf weeds in cereals.
- Keep insect pests under control by making sure no single type or group of crops are grown in succession.
- A mixture of winter- and spring-sown crops is best. Large blocks of a single crop should be avoided.
- Diverse crop rotations spread farm workload, reduce the risk of poor incomes and minimise the impact of any one crop on the environment.

The mosaic of different crops gives more diversity for wildlife, and some species benefit from the shifting pattern of crops from year to year. Varied crop rotations can also help improve soil structure[71].

What are the benefits of CA?
Suggested benefits include: reduced labour costs and reduced fuel usage, with the associated environmental benefits. Retention of crop residue at the surface (rather than ploughing it in), or cover crops reduce soil erosion by protecting the soil, as well as potentially providing winter food for birds. Less intense cultivation, and leaving crop residue at the surface can improve soil organic matter, and earthworm populations – whose activity can improve the porosity and drainage of the soil[45,51,54,59,72–74].

Are these benefits well recognised?
Yes. Some of the early work into conservation agriculture, called LIFE (Less Intensive Farming and Environment) study, ran from 1989 to 1994 and demonstrated reduced costs, as well as fertiliser and herbicide inputs[75]. In 1998 the Integrated Arable Crop Production Alliance produced a report looking at the forerunner to conservation agriculture[50], which concluded that integrated farming with minimum tillage:

- Reduced energy inputs
- Reduced nitrogen losses
- Improved physical properties of soil
- Allowed different weed control strategies
- Reduced the risk of soil erosion
- Increased beneficial plants and animals (biodiversity)
- Reduced the time to sow a crop by 52 minutes per hectare

Since 1998, much more research has been done into the effects of minimum/no tillage and conservation agriculture[51], and one study suggests that the benefits may be even greater when CA is applied on a wider scale than the results of smaller experiments can show. The improvements seem to be scale-dependent – larger areas under CA can give even larger improvements for soil erosion and water runoff than smaller areas[76].

How does CA save time?
Without ploughing, fewer passes across the field are needed, meaning less labour and less diesel. In a comparison of seven farms, five using non-inversion planting (CA), and two using a traditional mouldboard plough, on average the non-plough farms saved 52 minutes per hectare. This is equivalent to 6½ weeks work for a single man on a 300-hectare farm, with the accompanying lower fuel usage[49].

Why does CA reduce erosion?
For several reasons. We have observed at the Allerton Project that when soil is ploughed to a fine tilth (small, regular grains ideal for sowing crops), many small, free soil particles are formed, and these can easily be washed away, making their way to the drains through cracks in the soil. The reduced tillage component of CA eases this problem, and increases microbial soil health and earthworm abundance, which improves soil structure[57]. Cover crops reduce the impact with which rainfall hits the soil surface and reduce runoff[51].

Can we restore degraded soil to a good condition?
Usually yes, although it takes time. Incorporating organic material such as green manures and crop residues, introducing long crop rotations including a grass phase, planting cover crops in winter and reducing or eliminating ploughing, will help the soil to recover.

Does conservation agriculture have other effects on soil health?
Yes. SOWAP also provided strong evidence that soil microbes are often found in higher numbers with CA, compared to a conventional plough approach. The same kind of microbes are found, but there are more of them. Importantly, results from

71

SOWAP also suggested for the first time that improved microbial communities in soil can reduce the likelihood of soil erosion and improve moisture retention in summer[57].

Does this agree with other research?
Yes. It is widely accepted that no-till agriculture results in a better balance of microbes and other organisms, and therefore a healthier soil[17,51,77]. It is difficult to separate the effects of tillage alone from the other important components of CA, as they are often practiced together to give maximum benefits.

Is it easy to change to CA?
When planned properly it can be, but there can be pitfalls if the transition is not well managed – cultivation cannot be thought of in isolation, it is part of a greater management plan for the farm. Therefore, if cultivation management changes, other associated practices will need to be adjusted as well to match the new approach. For more details on planning a conversion to CA, refer to our website *www.gwct.org.uk/soilandwater* for useful resources.

Are there drawbacks to CA?
CA systems can have lower yields for some crops, and generally have increased weed pressure, at least when first established. CA is unsuitable for root crops and potatoes. Greater herbicide use may be needed to control weeds in the early years of conversion to CA, which often (but not always) eases as the new management systems become established. Despite reduced yields for some crops, operating costs are also reduced, therefore profit per hectare is similar[53]. Crop residues on the surface can lead to increased pressure from slugs, but there is evidence that sowing seed a little deeper than usual (around 4cm) can help reduce slug damage[78]. On a more general note, a conversion requires adaptability and attention to detail, combined with a good understanding of soils and technology, as well as a change in mindset.

So is CA the right approach?

CA can have many benefits, but it is important to choose a farming system that is suitable for local conditions, crops and climate. For example, adopting conservation agriculture on clay soils can be challenging.

Conservation Agriculture: Pros and Cons

Benefits:

- Improved soil structure
- Reduced water runoff
- Reduced erosion
- Improved soil biodiversity
- Increased number of earthworms
- Benefits to farmland birds
- Reduced fuel costs
- Reduced labour costs

Drawbacks:

- Planning a conversion – whole farm management approach that needs careful thought
- Increased pressure from weeds, especially reported in the early years after conversion
- Therefore, possible increased dependence on and cost of herbicides
- Yields of some crops are lower, although usually more than offset by reduced inputs
- CA is not always a suitable approach, and this is heavily affected by soil type

3.2 WATER FRIENDLY FARMING

The Water Friendly Farming project was designed to bring together the strands of knowledge described in this book, gained from many individual studies, applying it on a larger scale across the landscape, and investigate its effectiveness. It looks at a range of mitigation measures to reduce the impact of rural land use on ponds, streams and rivers, whilst not impacting the profitability of the farming business.

What is being done in Water Friendly Farming?
Water Friendly Farming is a large study conducted over three catchment areas in Leicestershire. They are all around 10km² in size, contain similar farming systems, soil types and landscape, and are drained by the Barkby Brook, the Eye Brook and the Stonton Brook. The study area is typical of a large part of the UK lowland farmed environment.

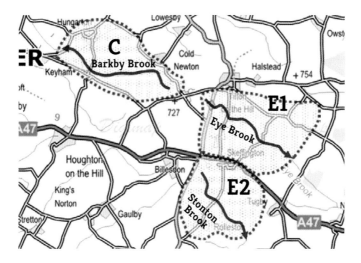

The Water Friendly Farming project is being conducted over three catchment areas in Leicestershire © GWCT

Why are there three study areas?

The Barkby Brook area was included for reference, where management was not changed. The other two catchments introduced methods to reduce the impacts of farming on water quality. These were designed to hold back sediments, nutrients and water, and increase the variety and abundance of freshwater wildlife across the study area.

What is Water Friendly Farming studying?

The project wants to answer three main questions:

1. Can we reduce diffuse water pollution?
2. Can we protect and increase freshwater biodiversity without reducing farm profitability?
3. Can we hold back water to help reduce downstream flooding?

Why is Water Friendly Farming important?
Water Friendly Farming is different to previous studies, because it looks at ways to reduce the impact of farming across whole catchments, rather than at a small (field or experimental plot) scale, as had previously been done. WFF also uses a robust experimental design, being what is known as a BACI, a Before-After-Control-Impact study. This means that three years of baseline data were collected on the study area before the interventions were put in place. There is also a "control", or reference site that is not altered to compare to, and this allows us to thoroughly assess the impact of the experiment. In other words, what do the interventions do collectively? It is an on-going project, giving enough time to assess the impact of what we are testing, despite weather variations.

What is measured in the Water Friendly Farming catchments?
Water quality in the streams at the base of each catchment is measured including phosphorus levels, nitrogen levels, and the amount of suspended sediment and pesticides.

What else is measured?
In 239 ponds, streams and ditches across the study areas, biodiversity is measured with surveys of wetland plants, freshwater invertebrates and water chemistry. Water flow is also monitored at the base of each of the three catchments.

What did the background monitoring show?
The baseline monitoring work was helpful in itself, revealing that:

- Ponds support the widest variety of freshwater species, despite representing the smallest area of water
- However, only about 10% of them were in good condition, with the majority either poor or very poor
- These ponds support some rare and sensitive freshwater plants, which are not found in any other water bodies in the region. One concern is that these plants showed

an apparent decline over the three monitoring years 2010-2013

- Streams in the study area have variable water quality. In each catchment there are sections of waterway that are "high" quality, meaning that they are clean, and sections that are moderate or poor quality
- Although all catchments had some patches of "clean" water, pollution was widespread, affecting around 95% of waterbodies
- Around 30% of waterbodies had low phosphorus levels, close to the natural background level
- Only around 5% of waterbodies had nitrogen levels that were near natural levels

What experimental methods are being tested?

Water management in the Eye Brook and Stonton Brook catchments has been altered to see if it improved water quality. No changes have been made to management in the Barkby Brook area. All catchments already had several buffer strips, mainly within agri-environment stewardship schemes. Dams and wetland interceptors in ditches were constructed in the Eye Brook catchment. These were also established in the Stonton Brook area, along with the additional creation of new clean water ponds (with surrounding buffers), and debris dams in some streams. More recently, permeable dams have been installed in the Eye Brook catchment to test the effect on flood risk downstream. These are log dams that do not affect water flow at normal levels, but will hold back excess flow during storm events when the water rises. An example is shown on the following page.

What do these techniques aim to do?

Buffer strips were added to slow and filter the water entering waterways from fields, trapping sediment and other pollutants before the water joined the stream/pond.

Dams, wetland interceptors and debris dams aim to slow the flow of water from ditches or field drains. With these features in place, there will be more time for sediment and associated nutrients to settle out before passing into the stream. Permeable dams are intended to trap flood water at times of extreme rainfall, aiming to reduce the downstream flow of water and reduce flood risk.

Permeable dams provide a simple, low-cost method of holding back excess flow during storm events © GWCT

If sediment is settling in these features, won't they fill up?
Yes, this is a sign that they are working, and the more sediment they are trapping, the faster they fill up. When they are full they can be dredged, and the sediment returned to the field.

What has Water Friendly Farming found so far?
Ponds
We knew from baseline monitoring that ponds are important for biodiversity, but that they are also more variable in terms of water quality than streams – because they are isolated, they can be very clean or very polluted, whereas because the water in streams is mixed, they tend to be less variable. WFF showed that establishing

new ponds improved freshwater biodiversity across the landscape[29]. This benefit for freshwater species was visible within a year of new ponds being established, giving a very quick improvement.

Buffer Strips
Buffer strips along or around water bodies can be effective for reducing sediment runoff, and computer modelling of WFF data suggested that buffer strips ten metres wide can reduce sediment loss by 30%, compared to standard buffer strips that are two metres wide[29].

Sediment loss
Computer models predicting the effect of farming techniques on erosion have shown that sediment loss could drop by 35-40% by switching to reduced or no-till farming[29].

Nutrient loss
Nitrogen and Phosphorus levels have shown trends across the three catchments that look mainly related to external factors, such as the weather. Phosphorus has shown a gradual increase and nitrogen a gradual decrease over the study[29].

Sewage works
All three of the project areas have small sewage works, as well as domestic septic tanks. Sewage treatment works dominate the phosphorus concentration at the base of the main catchments during normal conditions, for much of the year[42]. In small tributaries without sewage treatment works, the effect of land management can be seen more easily.

Flood risk
The study area is an arable landscape on clay soils, and very large volumes of water would need to be stored in the countryside to reduce flood risk. The features we installed can hold around 3000 cubic metres (this is a little more than one Olympic sized

swimming pool). Our computer analysis has suggested that this has had only a very slight effect on the amount of water flowing in rivers during wet weather. It also suggested that installing a network of 'permeable dams' could reduce the 1 in 100-year flood peak by 20%, and this work is currently underway in the area[29].

Pesticides
As well as picking up sediment and nutrients on its journey through farmland, water can also become contaminated with other chemicals, for example pesticides, that are used to treat crops. WFF looked at certain pesticides to understand this problem further and to provide a focus for discussion of broader issues with the participating farmers[79].

What is the most concerning pesticide for drinking water?
The most widespread threats to drinking water quality from pesticides comes from the active ingredient of slug pellets, metaldehyde and the herbicide propyzamide, which is used for control of black-grass within oil seed rape.

Do the water management techniques for reducing runoff and erosion also reduce metaldehyde in the water?
No. The measures we have tested have not had any real impact on concentrations in water, and we encourage farmers to substitute for a different product, ferric phosphate.

Do other pesticides contaminate watercourses?
Yes, as part of the Water Friendly Farming project, streams were also monitored for propyzamide and carbetamide. Propyzamide is a herbicide used for the control of black-grass. Results showed regular contamination of streams from November onwards. Carbetamide is also used to control grass weeds, but is much less widely used than propyzamide.

Is there an alternative treatment for black-grass?
There is no viable alternative herbicide for black-grass control in oil seed rape – propyzamide is the only effective herbicide for these crops. We have observed in some early work that buffer strips can help reduce propyzamide by up to 50%, but this needs further study (not yet published). Because burying black-grass seed underground for three years helps to control it, in some areas arable land is being sown to grass leys because of persistent problems. This has been a key driver for conversion of some fields to rotational grass at the Allerton Project.

Are there other measures for keeping propyzamide out of water?
Propyzamide binds to soil particles and often moves to water with soil, so reducing soil disturbance also reduces propyzamide runoff. Buffer strips, reducing the oilseed rape area, and increasing crop diversity also reduce propyzamide concentrations in water.

Discussion group

We recently used this herbicide as a focus for discussion of wider catchment and soil management issues with farmers[79]. Farmers were accepting of the need for buffer strips and identified benefits of vigorous hybrid barley for black-grass control, but identified the pitfalls associated with reducing the oilseed rape area across farms at the catchment scale. The discussion also highlighted the constraints on adopting a no-till system, including reduced yield, short-term tenure arrangements, continuing uncertainty about methods on clay soils, capital requirements, and political and economic uncertainty.
Continuing research at Loddington is designed to understand and address some of these issues.

4. Ongoing work at the Allerton Project

The continued research effort undertaken at Allerton and elsewhere has helped contribute much to our understanding soil and water on farms, how to reduce the impact of agriculture on these vital resources and how to move forward more sustainably. However, continued research is needed to fill in the gaps, and bring it all together. How do we farm profitably whilst encouraging healthy soils, clean water and biodiversity on farmland? Several projects are new or ongoing at Allerton to help with this picture:

Water Friendly Farming: The work described here is ongoing, giving time for the measures to become better established and allowing us to assess the true benefits and challenges of this landscape scale approach.

SoilCare: This is an EU Horizon 2020 funded project in which we are one of sixteen study sites across Europe, assessing how soil improving cropping systems improve the environmental and economic sustainability of soil management. Our local farmer network has played an important role in prioritising topics for research. We will be investigating methods for alleviating compaction, potential multiple benefits of grass leys, and the use of digestate from an anaerobic digestion plant for improving soil health and crop performance.

Soil Biology and Soil Health: This project is funded by AHDB (Agriculture and Horticulture Development Board) and the BBRO (British Beet Research Organisation) over five years, forming a partnership across sectors to focus on research and knowledge exchange. It is designed to help farmers and growers maintain and improve their productivity through a better understanding of soil biology and soil health. The Allerton Project is one of the study sites within the partnership where we will test the effect of ploughing long-term no-till land on soil biology and soil health as well as crop performance. This is an issue which visiting farmers who are considering no-till have raised with us as being a concern because of a possible need for periodic ploughing to control weeds.

For more information about our ongoing research, please visit *www.gwct.org.uk/allerton*

5. Summary – key points

- Deteriorating soil health is one of the biggest challenges facing farming, today and in the future
- Soil degradation is common and can occur because of erosion, compaction, loss of organic matter or contamination
- Water quality can be affected by contamination with nutrients, pesticides or sediment, and this is more likely where soil health is poor
- Current farming techniques can contribute to these problems, but scientific research is helping to find solutions that can ease the pressure on soils and water, whilst maintaining economically viable farming
- The Allerton Project has been a key player in soil and water research over the last 15 years
- Projects have examined individual techniques to reduce the impact of farming on soil and water, and help guide us into a more sustainable future for soils
- Ongoing projects follow on from this research, investigating sustainable solutions for the future, and combining several techniques into a landscape-scale demonstration.

6. Research projects

The Allerton Project has been involved in many research projects over the past 15 years, while maintaining and running a profitable farm business.

SOWAP (2003-2006)
Partners: Syngenta, Cranfield University, Freshwater Habitats Trust, RSPB
Aims: Examine the three main principles of conservation agriculture (CA) – reduced tillage, permanent soil cover and appropriate crop rotations. Assessed results achieved with both methods.
Findings: Conservation tillage reduced soil losses in areas that are vulnerable to erosion, and also reduced nitrogen runoff. CA was good for soil health – earth-worm and soil microbe populations generally increased, and birds preferred CA fields to conventional fields (although birds preferred overwinter stubbles even more). When looking at the effect of CA on the aquatic environments, results were very variable and we could not draw firm conclusions, but sediment loads were lower in streams draining CA areas. Yields for some crops were similar for both farming approaches, but for others, yields were lower from CA fields. This was often offset by lower costs with CA, so that profit remained comparable.

PARIS (2003-2008)
Partners: ADAS, CEH Wallingford, University of Leicester
Aims: Studying the concentration of nutrients in the stream passing through Loddington, and the Eye brook, running through pasture. Looking at bio-diversity in the stream with respect to nutrients, particularly phosphorus.
Findings: In terms of the total amount of phosphorus of all forms across the year in the study catchments, agriculture was the main source, being responsible for 67-99%, but other sources were also important. Phosphorus coming from farmland is highest in winter – when storms

wash sediment and phosphorus from fields. Other sources such as septic tanks, wastewater from buildings, animal waste from farm-yards and sewage works (called "point" sources) discharge phosphorus more steadily throughout the year, and have a greater ecological impact, even though the total annual amount is lower.

Aquatic insects such as damselfly benefited from dammed ditches and ditch-fed ponds © GWCT

WETTING UP FARMLAND FOR BIODIVERSITY (2004-2007)

Partners: RSPB, Freshwater Habitats Trust

Aims: Examining the importance for birds and other wildlife (e.g. insects) of wetland features on farmland: dammed drainage ditches, ditch-fed ponds, surface scrapes and waterlogged areas in livestock fields.

Findings: Dammed ditches and ditch-fed ponds were most effective, leading to production of more aquatic insects and visits from more birds.

MOPS1 (2005-2007)

Partners: Lancaster University

Aims: Investigate in-field approaches to reducing sediment and phosphorus losses from fields.

Findings: Tramlines are main source of sediment and phosphorus loss. Disrupting them reduced this in some areas, cultivating across the slope rather than up/down, and no-till farming did so in others.

Wetting up farmland for biodiversity – phase 2 (2008-2010)

Partners: RSPB, Freshwater Habitats Trust

Aims: Further studying the benefits of small scale wetland features on farmland, and examining the economic implications of these.

Findings: Field wetlands are beneficial for insects and birds on farmland. Larger features such as paired ponds are more effective than smaller ones. Dammed ditches need to be dredged approximately every 4 years. Dredging costs are estimated at approximately £10 per ditch per year.

MOPS2 (2009-2011)

Partners: Lancaster University

Aims: Investigate field wetlands for reducing sediment losses.

Findings: Field wetlands can trap a substantial amount of sediment in some circumstances on sand and silt soils, but are much less effective on clay soils.

Tramlines (2009-2013)

Partners: ADAS, Lancaster University, HGCA, NFU

Aims: To study the best way to reduce loss of water, sediment and nutrients along tramlines during autumn spraying operations. Sites at four farms across the UK with different soils.

Findings: Low pressure tyres and a rotary harrow fixed behind the tractor wheels to break up the surface of the soil are the most effective ways to reduce losses from tramlines. The harrow is most effective on all soils except for clay, where low pressure tyres are most effective. Using both approaches together is better still.

Water Friendly Farming (2011-2021)

Partners: Freshwater Habitats Trust, York University

Aims: Combine individual measures into a landscape-scale water management approach. Assess whether these techniques reduce the impact of farming on water quality.

Findings: Freshwater ponds are very important for biodiversity. Establishing new ponds quickly improved freshwater biodiversity across the landscape. Most water features across the landscape had raised nutrient levels. In areas with sewage works, these were the main source of phosphorus for most of the year. Current features will have little effect on downstream flood risk, so a network of permeable dams is being installed and tested.

Sustainable Intensification research Platform (SIP) (2014-2017)

Partners: NIAB, Nottingham University, York University

Aims: Studying techniques to improve sustainability in farming. Identify and develop farm management interventions for sustainably intensive agriculture.

Findings: At the Allerton Project, we studied the effect of different cover crop mixes compared to a bare stubble control. We looked at the chemistry, biology and physics of the soil, and the weed burden during the cover crop period and in the following crop. There were no differences between cover crop species for the soil analysis, but the cover crop species had a marked effect on earthworms and weed burden, with fewer weeds in radish. This weed suppression effect carried over into the subsequent crop, which gave a higher yield than in the absence of a previous cover crop. The project also enabled us to improve our understanding of the role of sward minerals in improving livestock performance on pasture and grass leys introduced into arable rotations to meet multiple objectives. Within the Water Friendly Farming project, the SIP enabled us to use a herbicide as a focus for discussion about practical opportunities and constraints for catchment management with participating farmers.

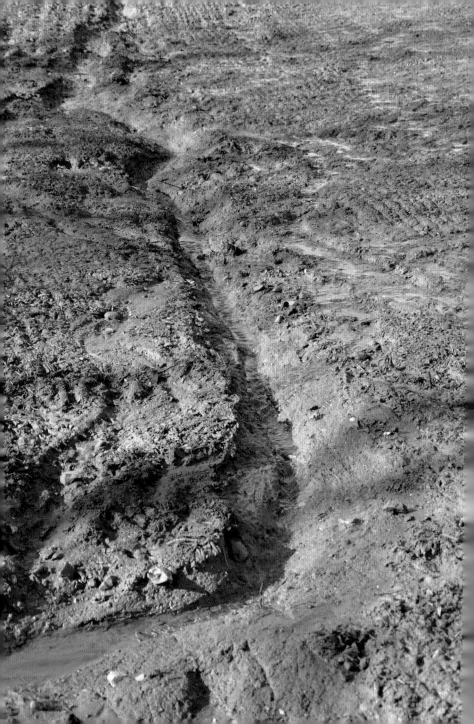

7. REFERENCES

1.   Thompson D. (2000) Soil Protection in the UK. Available at: https://www.soil-net.com/legacy/downloads/resources/hoc_soilprotection_briefing.pdf. (Accessed: 11th January 2018)

2.   Powlson DS, Gregory PJ, Whalley WR, Quinton JN, Hopkins DW, Whitmore AP, Hirsch PR & Goulding KWT. (2011) Soil management in relation to sustainable agriculture and ecosystem services. *Food Policy*, **36**: Supp 1

3.   Edwards AC & Withers PJA. (2008) Transport and delivery of suspended solids, nitrogen and phosphorus from various sources to freshwaters in the UK. J*ournal of Hydrology*, **350**: 144–153

4.   Biggs J, Stoate C, Williams P, Brown C, Casey A, Davies S, Diego IG, Hawczak A, Kizuka T, McGoff E & Szczur J. (2014). *Water Friendly Farming: Results and practical implications of the first 3 years of the programme.*

5.   Withers PJA, Jarvie HP & Stoate C. (2011) Quantifying the impact of septic tank systems on eutrophication risk in rural headwaters. *Environment International*, **37**: 644–653

6.   May L, Place C, O'Malley M & Spears B. (2015). *The impact of phosphorus inputs from small discharges on designated freshwater sites. Natural England Commissioned Reports, Number 170.*

7.   Doran JW & Zeiss MR. (2000) Soil health and sustainability: Managing the biotic component of soil quality. *Applied Soil Ecology,* **15**: 3–11

8.   Graves AR, Morris J, Deeks LK, Rickson RJ, Kibblewhite MG, Harris JA, Farewell TS & Truckle I. (2015) The total costs of soil degradation in England and Wales. *Ecological Economics*, **119**: 399–413

9.   Oldeman LR, Hakkeling RTA & Sombroek WG. (1991). *World Map of the Status of Human-Induced Soil Degradation: An Explanatory Note.*

10.   Batjes NH. (2014) Total carbon and nitrogen in the soils of the world. *European Journal of Soil Science*, **65**: 10–21

11.   Holden J, Haygarth PM, MacDonald J, Jenkins A, Sapiets A, Orr HG, Dunn N, Harris B, Pearson PL, McGonigle D, Humble A, Ross M, Harris J, Meacham T, Bento T, Staines A & Noble A. (2015). *Agriculture's impact on water quality.*

12.   Powlson DS, Whitmore AP & Goulding KWT. (2011) Soil carbon sequestration to mitigate climate change: A critical re-examination to identify the true and

the false. *European Journal of Soil Science*, **62**: 42–55

13. Minasny B, Malone BP, McBratney AB, Angers DA, Arrouays D, Chambers A, Chaplot V, Chen ZS, Cheng K, Das BS, Field DJ, Gimona A, Hedley CB, Hong SY, Mandal B, Marchant BP, Martin M, McConkey BG, Mulder VL, O'Rourke S, Richer-de-Forges AC, Odeh I, Padarian J, Paustian K, Pan G, Poggio L, Savin I, Stolbovoy V, Stockmann U, Sulaeman Y, Tsui CC, Vågen TG, van Wesemael B & Winowiecki L. (2017) Soil carbon 4 per mille. *Geoderma* **292**: 59–86

14. Bender SF, Wagg C & van der Heijden MGA. (2016) An Underground Revolution: Biodiversity and Soil Ecological Engineering for Agricultural Sustainability. *Trends in Ecology and Evolution* **31**: 440–452

15. Gans J, Wolinsky M & Dunbar J. (2005) logy: Computational improvements reveal great bacterial diversity and high toxicity in soil. *Science*, **309**: 1387–1390

16. Van Der Heijden MGA, Bardgett RD & Van Straalen NM. (2008) The unseen majority: Soil microbes as drivers of plant diversity and productivity in terrestrial ecosystems. *Ecology Letters* **11**: 296–310

17. Hobbs PR, Sayre K & Gupta R. (2008) The role of conservation agriculture in sustainable agriculture. *Philosophical transactions of the Royal Society of London. Series B, Biological sciences*, **363**: 543–55

18. Jones C, Basch G, Baylis A, Bazzoni D, Biggs J, Bradbury R, Chaney K, Deeks L, Field R, Gomez J, Jones R, Jordan V, Lane M, Leake A, Livermore M, Owens P, Ritz K, Sturny W & Thomas F. (2006). *Conservation Agriculture in Europe: An approch to sustainable crop production by protecting soil and water?*

19. Hudson BD. (1994) Soil organic matter and available water capacity. *Journal of Soil and Water Conservation*, **49**: 189–194

20. Stockfisch N, Forstreuter T & Ehlers W. (1999) Ploughing effects on soil organic matter after twenty years of conservation tillage in Lower Saxony, Germany. *Soil & Tillage Research*, **52**: 91–101

21. Van Groenigen JW, Lubbers IM, Vos HMJ, Brown GG, De Deyn GB & Van Groenigen KJ. (2014) Earthworms increase plant production: a meta-analysis. *Scientific Reports*, **4**: 6365

22. Emmerling C. (2001) Response of earthworm communities to different types of soil tillage. *Applied Soil Ecology*, **17**: 91–96

23. Bertrand M, Barot S, Blouin M, Whalen J, de Oliveira T & Roger-Estrade J. (2015) Earthworm services for cropping systems. A review. *Agronomy for Sustainable Development* **35**: 553–567

24. Reddy PP. (Springer Singapore, 2016). Agricultural Soil Compaction. in *Sustainable Intensification of Crop Production* 41–52 doi:10.1007/978-981-10-2702-4_3

25. Deasy C, Brazier RE, Heathwaite AL & Hodgkinson R. (2009) Pathways of runoff and sediment transfer in small agricultural catchments. *Hydrological Processes*, **23**: 1349–1358

26. Darmendrail D, Cerdan O, Gobin A, Bouzit M, Blanchard F & Siegele B. (2004). *Assessing the economic impact of soil deterioration: Case Studies and Database Research.*

27. Graves A, Morris J, Deeks L, Rickson J, Kibblewhite M, Harris J & Fairwell T. (2012). *The total costs of soil degradation in England and Wales. Final report to Defra project SP1606.*

28. Rickson RJ. (2014) Can control of soil erosion mitigate water pollution by sediments? *Science of the Total Environment*, **468–469**: 1187–1197

29. Biggs J, Stoate C, Williams P, Brown C, Casey A, Davies S, Diego IG, Hawczak A, Kizuka T, McGoff E, Szczur J & Velez MV. (2016). *Water Friendly Farming: Autumn 2016 update.*

30. AHDB. (2015). *Field drainage guide: principles, installation and maintenance.*

31. Bilotta GS & Brazier RE. (2008) Understanding the influence of suspended solids on water quality and aquatic biota. *Water Research* **42**: 2849–2861

32. Newcombe CP & MacDonald D. (1991) Effects of suspended sediments on aquatic ecosystems. *North American Journal of Fisheries Management*, **11**: 72–82

33. Kemp P, Sear D, Collins A, Naden P & Jones I. (2011) The impacts of fine sediment on riverine fish. *Hydrological Processes*, **25**: 1800–1821

34. Suttle KB, Power ME, Levine JM & McNeely C. (2004) How fine sediment in riverbeds impairs growth and survival of juvenile salmonids. *Ecological Applications*, **14**: 969–974

35. Sear DA, Jones JI, Collins AL, Hulin A, Burke N, Bateman S, Pattison I & Naden PS. (2016) Does fine sediment source as well as quantity affect salmonid embryo mortality and development? *Science of the Total*

Environment, **541**: 957–968

36. Stubbing DN. (King's College London, 2009). A study of brown trout, Salmo trutta L., egg survival and intra-gravel ecology in livestock catchments with farm management plans to mitigate against diffuse pollution.

37. Summers DW, Giles N & Willis DJ. (1996). *Restoration of riverine trout habitats: A guidance manual.*

38. Meyer EI, Niepagenkemper O, Molls F & Spänhoff B. (2008) An experimental assessment of the effectiveness of gravel cleaning operations in improving hyporheic water quality in potential salmonid spawning areas. *River Research and Applications*, **24**: 119–131

39. Potter ECE & Dare CJ. (2003). *Research on migratory salmonids, eels and freshwater fish stocks and fisheries.*

40. Harper DM. (Springer, 1992). *Eutrophication of Fresh Waters.*

41. Collins AL & Anthony SG. (2008) Assessing the likelihood of catchments across England and Wales meeting 'good ecological status' due to sediment contributions from agricultural sources. *Environmental Science and Policy*, **11**: 163–170

42. Jarvie HP, Withers PJA, Bowes MJ, Palmer-Felgate EJ, Harper DM, Wasiak K, Wasiak P, Hodgkinson RA, Bates A, Stoate C, Neal M, Wickham HD, Harman SA & Armstrong LK. (2010) Streamwater phosphorus and nitrogen across a gradient in rural-agricultural land use intensity. *Agriculture, Ecosystems and Environment*, **135**: 238–252

43. Defra. (2008). *Linking agricultural land use and practices with a high risk of phosphorus loss to chemical and ecological impacts in rivers (PE0116 and WT0705CSF).*

44. European Commission. (2010). *EU Nitrates Directive.*

45. Crotty F V., Fychan R, Sanderson R, Rhymes JR, Bourdin F, Scullion J & Marley CL. (2016) Understanding the legacy effect of previous forage crop and tillage management on soil biology, after conversion to an arable crop rotation. *Soil Biology and Biochemistry*, **103**: 241–252

46. Pagliai M, Vignozzi N & Pellegrini S. (2004). Soil structure and the effect of management practices. in *Soil and Tillage Research* **79**: 131–143

47. Riley H, Pommeresche R, Eltun R, Hansen S & Korsaeth A. (2008) Soil structure, organic matter and earthworm activity in a comparison of cropping systems with contrasting tillage, rotations, fertilizer levels and

manure use. *Agriculture, Ecosystems and Environment*, **124**: 275–284

48. Montgomery DR. (2007) Soil erosion and agricultural sustainability. *Proceedings of the National Academy of Sciences of the United States of America*, **104**: 13268–72

49. Leake A & Lane M. (2009). Soil and Water Project (SOWAP) - So What? in *Global Change- Challenges for Soil Management. International Conference for Land Conservation*. 213–217

50. MAFF. (1998). *Integrated farming: Agricultural research into practice.*

51. Holland JM. (2004) The environmental consequences of adopting conservation tillage in Europe: Reviewing the evidence. *Agriculture, Ecosystems and Environment* **103**: 1–25

52. Schoumans OF, Chardon WJ, Bechmann ME, Gascuel-Odoux C, Hofman G, Kronvang B, Rubæk GH, Ulén B & Dorioz JM. (2014) Mitigation options to reduce phosphorus losses from the agricultural sector and improve surface water quality: A review. *Science of the Total Environment*, **468–469**: 1255–1266

53. Van den Putte A, Govers G, Diels J, Gillijns K & Demuzere M. (2010) Assessing the effect of soil tillage on crop growth: A meta-regression analysis on European crop yields under conservation agriculture. *European Journal of Agronomy*, **33**: 231–241

54. Field RH, Kirby WB & Bradbury RB. (2007) Conservation tillage encourages early breeding by Skylarks Alauda arvensis. *Bird Study*, **54**: 137–141

55. Saunders H. (2000) Bird species as indicators to assess the impact of integrated crop management on the environment: a comparative study. *Aspects of Applied Biology*, **62**: 47–53

56. Rothwell AJ. (Harper Adams University College, 2007). The impact of non-inversion tillage and mouldboard ploughing on earthworm numbers, biomass and species.

57. Allton K. (Cranfield, 2006). Interactions between soil microbial communities, erodability and tillage practices.

58. SOWAP. (2007). *Soil and surface water protection using conservation tillage in northern and central Europe (SOWAP). LIFE03 ENV/UK/000617 Technical Final Report.*

59. Cunningham HM, Bradbury RB, Chaney K & Wilcox A. (2005) Effect of

non-inversion tillage on field usage by UK farmland birds in winter. *Bird Study*, **52**: 173–179

60.   Crotty F & Stoate C. (2017) Understanding cover crops at the farm-scale - a method of sustainable intensification? *Aspects of Applied Biology*, **136**: 79–86

61.   Dabney SM, Delgado JA & Reeves DW. (2001) Using winter cover crops to improve soil and water quality. *Communications in Soil Science and Plant Analysis*, **32**: 1221–1250

62.   Hartwig NL & Ammon HU. (2002) 50th Anniversary — Invited Article Cover crops and living mulches. *Weed Science*, **50**: 688–699

63.   Lee M, Stoate C, Crotty F, Kendall N, Rivero J, Williams P, Chadwick D, Stobart R, Morris N, Butler G, Takahashi T, McAuliffle G & Orr R. (2017). SIP Project 1: *Integrated Farm Management for Improved Economic, Environmental and Social Performance (LM0201).*

64.   Deasy C, Quinton J, Silgram M, Bailey A, Jackson B & Stevens C. (2009) Mitigation Options for Sediment and Phosphorus Loss from Winter-sown Arable Crops. *Journal of Environment Quality*, **38**: 2121

65.   Deasy C, Quinton J, Silgram M, Jackson B, Bailey A & Stevens C. (2008). *Defra PE0206 Field Testing of Mitigation Options.*

66.   Silgram M, Jackson B, McKenzie B, Quinton J, Williams D, Harris D, Lee D, Wright P, Shanahan P & Zhang Y. (2015). *Reducing the risks associated with autumn wheeling of combinable crops to mitigate runoff and diffuse pollution: a field and catchment scale evaluation. Defra project report no. 559.*

67.   Ockenden MC, Deasy C, Quinton JN, Bailey AP, Surridge B & Stoate C. (2012) Evaluation of field wetlands for mitigation of diffuse pollution from agriculture: Sediment retention, cost and effectiveness. *Environmental Science and Policy*, **24**: 110–119

68.   Newman J, Duenas-Lopez M, Acreman M, Palmer-Felgate E, Verhoeven J, Scholz M & Maltby E. (2015). *Do on-farm natural, restored, managed and constructed wetlands mitigate agricultural pollution in Great Britain and Ireland? A systematic review. Defra.*

69.   Defra. Wetting up Farmland for Birds and other Biodiversity (BD1323). Available at: http://randd.defra.gov.uk/Default.aspx?Menu=Menu&Module=More&Location=None&Completed=0&ProjectID=13053

70.   Defra. Wetting up Farmland for biodiversity (phase 2, BD1326). Available at: http://sciencesearch.defra.gov.uk/Default.aspx?Menu=Menu&Module=More&Location=None&Completed=0&ProjectID=14809.

71.   Munkholm LJ, Heck RJ & Deen B. (2013) Long-term rotation and tillage effects on soil structure and crop yield. *Soil and Tillage Research*, **127**: 85–91

72.   Field RH, Benke S, Bádonyi K & Bradbury RB. (2007) Influence of conservation tillage on winter bird use of arable fields in Hungary. *Agriculture, Ecosystems and Environment*, **120**: 399–404

73.   Leys A, Govers G, Gillijns K & Poesen J. (2007) Conservation tillage on loamy soils: Explaining the variability in interrill runoff and erosion reduction. *European Journal of Soil Science*, 58: 1425–1436

74.   Crotty F V., Fychan R, Scullion J, Sanderson R & Marley CL. (2015) Assessing the impact of agricultural forage crops on soil biodiversity and abundance. *Soil Biology and Biochemistry*, **91**: 119–126

75.   Jordan VWL, Hutcheon JA, Donaldson G V. & Farmer DP. (1997) Research into and development of integrated farming systems for less-intensive arable crop production: Experimental progress (1989-1994) and commercial implementation. *Agriculture, Ecosystems and Environment*, **64**: 141–148

76.   Leys A, Govers G, Gillijns K, Berckmoes E & Takken I. (2010) Scale effects on runoff and erosion losses from arable land under conservation and conventional tillage: The role of residue cover. *Journal of Hydrology*, **390**: 143–154

77.   Stockdale E & Watson C. (2012). *Managing soil biota to deliver ecosystem services. Natural England Commissioned Reports, Number 100.*

78.   Glen D. (2002) Integrated control of slug damage. *Pesticide Outlook*, **13**: 137–141

79.   Stoate C, Brown C, Velez M., Jarratt S, Morris C, Biggs J, Szczur J & Crotty F. (2017) The use of a herbicide to investigate catchment management approaches to meeting Sustainable Intensification (SI) objectives. *Aspects of Applied Biology*, **136**: 115–120

About GWCT

THE HOME OF WORKING CONSERVATION

The Game & Wildlife Conservation Trust is the home of working conservation. We believe that wildlife can thrive if we focus on integrating it alongside other land uses.

From producing food to providing space for nature, we understand these need to happen in the same place. To balance these needs we use our outcomes approach, and its importance is growing. We live on a small busy island and the demands we place on our countryside increase as our population grows and we add new outcomes, such as recreation and clean air.

Gamekeepers became the unexpected champions of the outcomes approach as farming modernised to meet the post-war demand for food. The GWCT carefully studied how they began to use their range of tools, from trapping to growing small strips of cover crop, to maintain their bird numbers without hindering farm production. Today these gamekeeping techniques are vital conservation tools – because they support wildlife into a working countryside.

Find out more about the GWCT and support us at **www.gwct.org.uk**.